I, B.C.

by

Johnny Hart

FAWCETT GOLD MEDAL • NEW YORK

I, B.C.

Published by Fawcett Gold Medal Books, a unit of
CBS Publications, the Consumer Publishing Division
of CBS Inc.

ISBN: 0-449-14313-9

Printed in the United States of America

First Fawcett Gold Medal printing: January 1980

10   9   8   7   6   5   4   3   2   1

5.8

OK, THOR, TODAY YOU'RE THE DESIGNATED HITTER AND THIRD-BASE COACH.

5·13

HOWEVER, IF PETER GETS ON, YOU'LL GO IN AS A RUNNER—UNLESS HE STRETCHES IT INTO A TRIPLE—IN WHICH CASE YOU'LL WARM UP TO RELIEVE CLUMSY IF HE DOESN'T HAVE HIS STUFF.

WHO'S GONNA BLOW ON THE FLAG DURING THE STAR SPANGLED BANNER?

hart

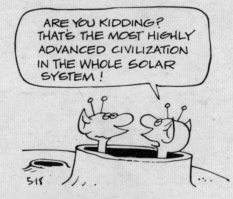

5·27

5-28

5·29

6·12

I'M AFRAID I'VE REFINED THE WHEEL AS FAR AS HUMANLY POSSIBLE.

6·21

THAT SHOULD BE GOOD NEWS TO THE CHIMPS.

6·22

6-26

ANYBODY WANNA BUY
A SEAT IN THE END-ZONE
FOR HALF PRICE?

71

7-3

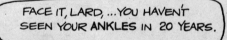

7·8

7.10

7.12

GOLF

7.13

IF YOU DON'T SHOW ME HOW TO CORRECT MY SLICE, I'M QUITTING THIS **STUPID** GAME!

LET ME SEE YOUR SWING.

PRO SHOP

7-16

7-22

7-23

SPEED
LIMIT
55

7-24

ME **BOY**!.... YOU **GIRL**!

7-31

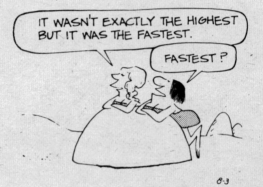

8-3

8-9

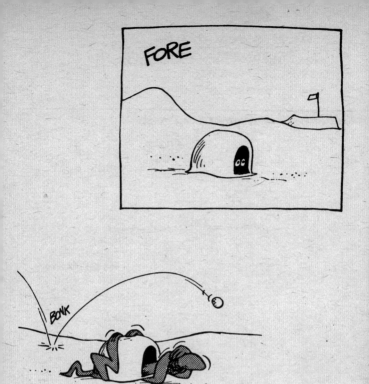

8-15

8·23

8-24

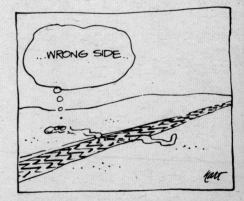

9.3

TUMBLEWEEDS GOT LEGS!

BLINK
  BLINK
BLINKITY
   BLINK
  BLINK
   BLINK
 BLINK BLINK

10-12